Classical Syncs

for two violins

book one

arranged by Myanna Harvey

CHP320

©2017 by C. Harvey Publications All Rights Reserved.

www.charveypublications.com - print books

www.learnstrings.com - downloadable books

Classical Syncs for Two Violins Book One

all duets arranged by Myanna Harvey

Table of Contents

	Title	Page
1.	**Allegro from** *Concerto Grosso in d minor, RV565* (Antonio Vivaldi)	2
2.	**Adagio** from *Concerto Grosso No. 8* (Christmas Concerto) (Arcangelo Corelli)	4
3.	**Slavonic Dance No. 8**: *Furiant* (Antonin Dvorak)	6
4.	**Allegro** from *Night Music of the Streets of Madrid* (Luigi Boccherini)	8
5.	**Chanson de Matin** (Edward Elgar)	10
6.	**Allegro** from the *Water Music* (George Frideric Handel)	12
7.	**The Moldau** from *Ma Vlast* (Bedrich Smetana)	14
8.	**Adagio** from *Concerto BWV 1060R* (Johann Sebastian Bach)	16
9.	**Allegro** from *Concerto BWV 1060R* (Johann Sebastian Bach)	18
10.	**Dance of the Tumblers** from *The Snow Maiden* (Nikolai Rimsky-Korsakov)	20
11.	**Allegro** from *Sonata in G, K 427* (Domenico Scarlatti)	22
12.	**Golliwog's Cakewalk** (Claude Debussy)	24
13.	**Jupiter** from *The Planets* (Gustav Holst)	26
14.	**Intermezzo** from *Cavalleria Rusticana* (Pietro Mascagni)	28

Classical Syncs; Duets for Two Violins, Book One

from the 17th through the 20th Centuries

Allegro from *Concerto Grosso in d minor*, RV 565

A. Vivaldi, arr. M. Harvey

©2017 C. Harvey Publications All Rights Reserved.

Classical Syncs; Duets for Two Violins, Book One

Adagio from the *Christmas Concerto*

A. Corelli, arr. M. Harvey

©2017 C. Harvey Publications All Rights Reserved.

This page is left blank to eliminate page turns.

Slavonic Dance No. 8: Furiant

A. Dvorak, arr. M. Harvey

Classical Syncs; Duets for Two Violins, Book One

©2017 C. Harvey Publications All Rights Reserved.

Allegro from *Night Music of the Streets of Madrid*

Allegro Vivo
L. Boccherini, arr. M. Harvey

Classical Syncs; Duets for Two Violins, Book One

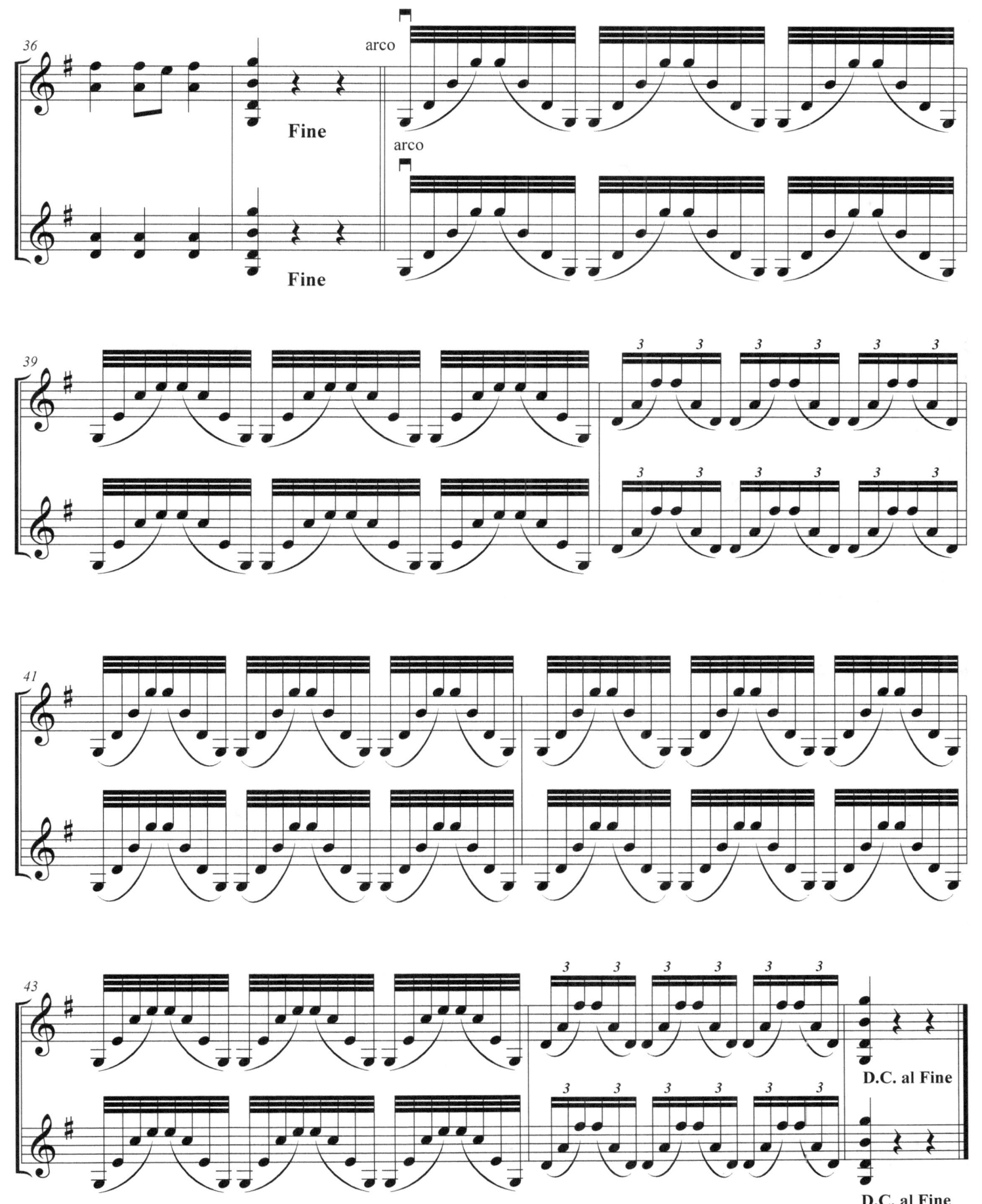

©2017 C. Harvey Publications All Rights Reserved.

Chanson de Matin

E. Elgar, arr. M. Harvey

Classical Syncs; Duets for Two Violins, Book One

©2017 C. Harvey Publications All Rights Reserved.

Allegro from *The Water Music*

G. F. Handel, arr. M. Harvey

Classical Syncs; Duets for Two Violins, Book One

The Moldau from Ma Vlast

B. Smetana, arr. M. Harvey

Classical Syncs; Duets for Two Violins, Book One

15

Adagio from Concerto BWV 1060R

J. S. Bach, arr. M. Harvey

Classical Syncs; Duets for Two Violins, Book One

17

©2017 C. Harvey Publications All Rights Reserved.

Allegro from Concerto BWV 1060R

J. S. Bach, arr. M. Harvey

Classical Syncs; Duets for Two Violins, Book One 19

Dance of the Tumblers from *The Snow Maiden*

N. Rimsky-Korsakov, arr. M. Harvey

Classical Syncs; Duets for Two Violins, Book One

Allegro from *Sonata in G*, K 427

D. Scarlatti, arr. M. Harvey

Golliwog's Cakewalk

Allegro giusto

C. Debussy, arr. M. Harvey

Classical Syncs; Duets for Two Violins, Book One
25

©2017 C. Harvey Publications All Rights Reserved.

Jupiter from *The Planets*

G. Holst, arr. M. Harvey

Intermezzo from *Cavalleria Rusticana*

P. Mascagni, arr. M. Harvey

Classical Syncs; Duets for Two Violins, Book One

Was this book helpful?
We would love it if you left a review where you bought it!

Not so helpful?
We're happy to hear any feedback. Was the book what you expected from what we described? If not, let us know how we can describe it better. Or, let us know how the book could be more helpful to you. Just send an email with your comments or questions to info@charveypublications.com.

Many more print study books and duets are available at
www.charveypublications.com.

Downloadable study books and duets are available at
www.learnstrings.com.

Don't see what you need?
Send us an email suggesting a book: info@charveypublications.com. While we regret that we cannot write a book for every suggestion, we do use customer feedback to help determine which books to publish next. Some of our most popular books were written in response to customer suggestions!

www.ingramcontent.com/pod-product-compliance
Lightning Source LLC
Chambersburg PA
CBHW051430070526
44584CB00023B/3655